AUSTRIA

TIGER BOOKS INTERNATIONAL

Text by
Carlo Belihar

Graphic design
Patrizia Balocco

Map
Arabella Lazzarin

Contents

When the Mountain is Your Friend........................ *page*   26
Vienna, the Grandeur of the Empire.................... *page*   62
The Smaller Cities.. *page*   98

1 *An art nouveau frieze bedecks the metro station of Karlsplatz, in Vienna.*

2-3 *The castle of Schönbrunn, seen from the Gloriette. The initial project as conceived by Johann Bernhard Fischer von Erlach called for a sort of "super-Versailles". But the empress Maria Theresa found the project to be too costly, and made do with what you see here.*

4-5 *This photograph shows Innsbruck from the top of the Olympic diving board at Igls.*

6-7 *All the charm of Salzburg, under a blanket of snow. The domes of the belltowers and of the cathedral are seen in the centre; in the foreground is the Collegiate.*

8 *The Anker Uhr is a great clock with carillon, featuring a procession of figures representing great personages from the past. It is located in Vienna, on the Hoher Markt, where the old city once stood.*

9 *This statue of Minerva wielding her lance stands before the Austrian parliament on the Ring. Often, the Viennese complain that the goddess of reason seems to be relegated outside, rather than on the interior of the elegant building.*

12-13 *The morning chill envelops the Gaschurn in Montafon. The ski resorts of Vorarlberg are somewhat less a meeting place for high society than those in the Tyrol and the Salzburg area.*

14-15 *The earliest rays of sunlight slant over the Wildspitze in Ötztal. The Tyrolean mountains are an earthly paradise for skiers.*

16-17 *In Austria, castles are scattered just about everywhere. The thirteenth-century manor of Waldenstein is perched upon the Koralpe in Styria, not far from the deep forest hot springs of Sankt Leonhard, and near the stud farm at Piber, where the famous Lippizaner show horses, used in dressage, are bred.*

This edition published in 1994 by TIGER BOOKS INTERNATIONAL PLC , 26a York Street Twickenham TW1 3LJ, England.

First published by Edizioni White Star. Title of the original edition: India, un viaggio nel Paese dello spirito. © World copyright 1994 by Edizioni White Star, Via Candido Sassone 22/24, 13100 Vercelli, Italy.

ISBN 1-85501-476-9

Printed in Singapore by Tien Wah Press. Color separations by Magenta, Lit. Con., Singapore.

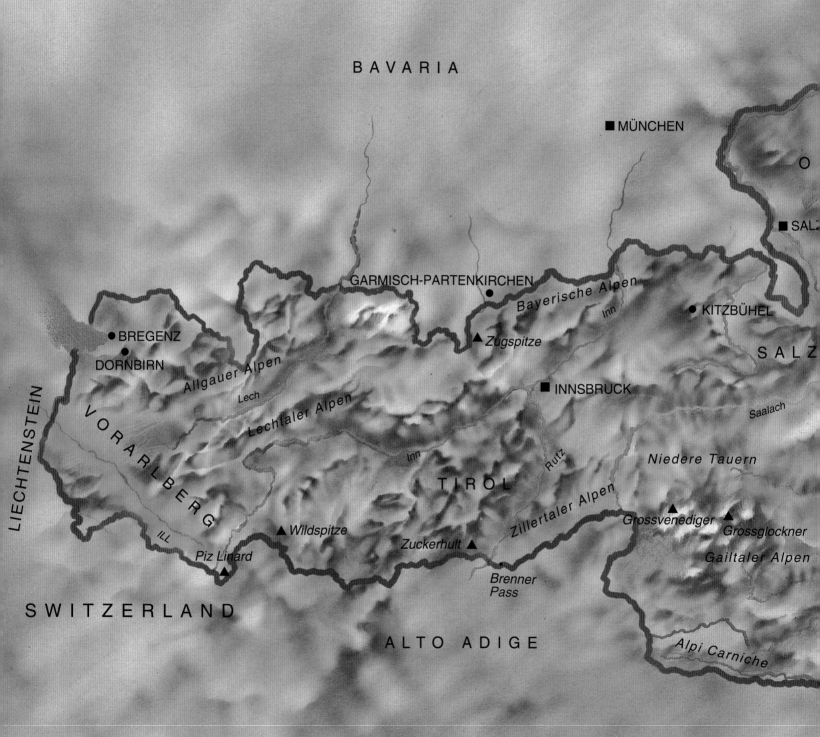

GERMANY

BAVARIA

■ MÜNCHEN

O

■ SALZ

GARMISCH-PARTENKIRCHEN
●

Bayerische Alpen

Inn

● KITZBÜHEL

▲ Zugspitze

● BREGENZ

● DORNBIRN

Allgauer Alpen

SALZ

Lech

Lechtaler Alpen

■ INNSBRUCK

Saalach

LIECHTENSTEIN

VORARLBERG

Inn

Rutz

Niedere Tauern

TIROL

Zillertaler Alpen

ILL

▲ Wildspitze

Grossvenediger ▲

▲

Piz Linard

Zuckerhult ▲

Grossglockner

▲

Brenner
Pass

Gailtaler Alpen

SWITZERLAND

ALTO ADIGE

Alpi Carniche

ITALY

CZECH REPUBLIC

NIEDERÖSTERREICH

ÖSTERREICH

SLOVAKIA

HUNGARY

Danube

Aist

Lainsitz

Thaya

LINZ

Traun

VIENNA

Danube

Leitha

d Lake

Atter Lake

Ybbs

BURGENLAND

Traisen

Neusiedl Lake

RG

Enns

R

Hohe Tauern

STEIERMARK

Mürz

Lafnitz

GRAZ

Raab

Mur

Lavant

Hochalm-Sp.

Lieser

KARNTEN

KLAGENFURT

Drau

VILLACH

Wörther Lake

Karawanken Alpen

SLOVENIA

Introduction

Two great lakes spread glittering at the westernmost and easternmost borders of Austria: Lake Constance, in the western province of Vorarlberg, and Lake Neusiedl, in the eastern province of Burgenland. Both these lakes share at least one common feature: a floating stage. The floating stage at Bregenz, on Lake Constance, is used for performances of grand opera, while the stage at Mörbisch is used for operetta, or light opera. The architectural forms that are found in Austria range widely: from the sharp belltowers typical of the Reformation, along the border with Germany and Switzerland, all the way to the rounded domes dating from the Counter Reformation in Salzburg and Vienna, and on, to the far end of the spectrum, with the spectacular proliferation of interlocking vaults found in the Bergkirche in Eisenstadt, capital of the eastern province of Burgenland. The latter style of architecture is in some ways reminiscent of the work of the sixteenth-century Turkish architect Sinan, a great builder of mosques. Austria, in short, has a bit of everything.

Not unlike certain ladies with a glorious past, whose brilliance may have been burnished by time, Austria does not dazzle at first glance. The better one knows the country, however, the deeper the attraction. To those who have the patience to study Austria, vast horizons open out, horizons of spirituality, culture, lifelong experience, and mutual understanding that do not emerge at first blush. Austria carries the weight of an artistic and historical heritage that its understated agrarian countryside tends, in some sense, to conceal; nonetheless, this heritage emerges in the most unlooked-for ways.

A small lake, the tiny Hintersee, with its stand of pines that could pass for a stretch of Canadian forest, continues to harbour chattering ducks just a few miles from the cupolas and spires of Salzburg, from the staircase by Lucas von Hildebrandt at Mirabell, from the altar carved by Michael Pacher in Sankt Wolfgang, from the Roman theatre on the shore of the little manmade lake in the castle of Hellbrunn, where an archbishop during the Baroque period ordered a statue of Marcus Aurelius placed amongst two groups of marble statues of slaves. And yet, and yet...the link is there. Marcus Aurelius died fourteen centuries before that archbishop lived, in the Roman military outpost of *Vindobona*, now known as Vienna.

There is no beginning or end to Austria's past. At Willendorf, near Baden, archaeologists have uncovered a terracotta Venus dating from the fifteenth millennium B.C. And in Vienna, seven centuries ago, the first bank collapse - bankruptcy, literally - took place. Leopold VI of Babenburg had founded a credit bank, in order to provide some competition to the usurers, but he was rapidly forced to cease operations due to interference from the church. *Nihil sub Sole Novi?*

A great many races and peoples have passed through this region. Each of them has left an hereditary imprint of one sort of another, beginning with the Indo-Germanic tribes of the Stone Age. While the first pan-Hellenic games were being held at Olympia, and while Romulus and Remus were quarrelling over just where to lay down the boundaries of Rome, the mythical Illyrians and Celts were making their way across the Austrian landscape. In 101 B.C., Gaius Marius defeated the Cimbri, and thereafter he established the *Limes*, an ancient Roman frontier fortification, upon the Danube - a boundary that held fast for seven centuries. *Carnuntum* and *Vindobona* had all the time the two settlements needed to develop from military camps into urban entities. With time, *Carnuntum* disappeared, and *Vindobona* survived and prospered. While Roman troops were laying siege to Jerusalem in A.D. 70, just prior to the destruction of the city, a legion from Syria was transferred to the banks of the Danube: a remarkable transfer, ordered by prudent Roman commanders who felt they could not count upon the legion's loyalty. With that legion came the cult of Mithras, a Persian religion to whose secret rituals only men were initiated, the most vital competitor of Christianity throughout the Roman empire in the second and third centuries A.D. Amidst the ruins of *Carnuntum*, once headquarters to the Roman legate, or provincial governor, of Pannonia - a province in the east that stretches from the Wienerwald, or Vienna woods, all the way to Budapest - one can visit an eight-thousand-seat amphitheatre, and a great complex of thermal baths, a favoured meeting place for Roman dignitaries and businessmen, a refuge from the chilly winds that gust between the Danube and the *puszta*. In response to the growing pressure of the barbarians upon the Roman frontier, Gregory the Great, the late-sixth-century saint and pope, sent armies of preachers and missionaries to this area. In place of fortifications, great convents were built along the Danube River and between the mountainous buttresses: the abbey of Klosterneuburg, as imposing as an Escorial before its time; the abbey of Göttweig; the superb abbey of Melk, a baroque jewel set overlooking the Wachau; Sankt Florian, the abbey that was so dear to Anton Bruckner; Heilingenkreuz in the Wienerwald; Admont in the metalliferous Alps of Styria, a province in southeastern Austria; and Sankt Paul in Lavanthal in the province of Carinthia. These were the fortresses from which Christianity sallied forth to defeat the pagans: built upon solidly fortified foundations, with walls that reared straight up above tumbling rivers or deep valleys, topped by battlements. Graceful baroque constructions were added, centuries later, set upon stone arches that refused to collapse.

Until the turn of the second century, no known surviving document mentioned Austria. The name *Ostarrichi* was penned for the first time in a document emanated by the Holy Roman Emperor Otto III in A.D. 996. Till that time, the region was considered to be merely the "eastern march" of the Holy Roman Empire, newly invented by the Germans. Otto had bestowed the "march" in question to count Luitpold of Babenberg, in return for Luitpold's faithful service.

The Babenbergs remained in *Ostarrichi* for two hundred and seventy years, expanding their territory

18 *The superb Benedictine abbey of Melk overlooks the Danube from atop a huge crag towering nearly two hundred feet tall. It was built in the eleventh century as the fortress of Leopold of Babenberg, and was subsequently enlarged and renovated by Jakob Prandtauer and Josef Munggenast during the first decades of the eighteenth century. This castle is one of the most important works of baroque art and architecture in all of Europe, and possesses a major library.*

eastward into Bohemia and Hungary. They met their end at the hands of the Hungarians. The last of the Babenbergs, Federick the Quarrelsome, was killed in a "victorious battle" near Wiener-Neustadt. Six centuries later, the emperor Franz Josef (Francis Joseph) I came very close to being stabbed to death by an Hungarian tailor. In thanksgiving for his survival, a votive church -- the Votivkirche - was built in Vienna. And so the Austrian region fell under the rule of the Hapsburgs, with their policy of alliances and politically motivated marriages, a policy that was celebrated by a poet of the imperial court with the lines: *Bella gerant alii, tu felix Austria nube*, meaning "Let others wage (ruinous) wars, (while) you, blessed Austria, accept marriage." Other scholars attribute this saying to Emperor Maximilian I himself.

The Hapsburgs ruled for six-and-a-half centuries: first as Holy Roman Emperors, and thereafter, following the conquest of Vienna by Napoleon Bonaparte, as Emperors of Austria, Kings of Hungary and Bohemia, Dalmatia, Croatia, Slavonia, Galicia, Lodomiria, and Illyria, and as Lords of Trieste. Although the Hapsburgs waged a great many wars, the dizzying expansion of their power was solidified and crowned above all through political marriages that consolidated personal and patrimonial relationships. Maximilian I was the unrivalled champion in this field. Tyrolean, roguish, bellicose, energetic, and at the same time quite generous, Maximilian succeeded in founding with his three great "matrimonial complexes" a political edifice that survived for centuries. First of all, by marrying in 1477 Mary of Burgundy, the daughter of Charles the Bold of Burgundy, Maximilian extended his imperial power over all of the *Franche-Comté*, establishing a foothold in the Low Countries with the "Wedding of Burgundy". Then, taking as his second wife Bianca Maria Sforza, the niece of Lodovico Sforza, known as Lodovico Il Moro, or The Moor, he reinforced his presence in Italy, though he was thus caught up in the Italian Wars. With the "Spanish Marriage" of 1496, he wed his son Philip the Handsome to Joanna of Castile and Aragon, the daughter of Ferdinand of Aragon and Isabella of Castile. Joanna went mad when Philip died. At the same time, Margaret of Austria, the daughter of Maximilian, married first John of Spain and, after he died, Philibert I of Savoy. She then became the guardian of her nephew - the son of Philip the Handsome and the future Holy Roman Emperor Charles V.

The third step in this amazing series of politically astute marriages was the "Marriage of Bohemia and Hungary". The grandchildren of Maximilian - Ferdinand and Mary of Hapsburg - married, respectively, Ann of Hungary and Bohemia, and Ludwig of Hungary and Bohemia. Suffice this brief account, then, to explain why in Austria, more than in so many other countries, tourists are automatically captured by the monumental display of historical landmarks and monuments.

The same sort of thing may happen in Italy, France, or England, but never in the absorbing, entrancing way that it does in Austria. Since the Hapsburgs were fruitful and multiplied, the term "House of Austria" was used to designate the family, and the details of this household are astonishing: four Kings of the Germans, fifteen Holy Roman Emperors, six Kings of Spain and - following the conquest of Vienna by

19 top The Cistercian abbey of Stams was built in the high valley of the River Inn at the behest of Elizabeth of Bavaria, the widow of the Emperor Conrad IV of Swabia, who was decapitated in Naples in 1268. In the crypt of the abbey the remains of a number of rulers are buried; among them are the bones of Bianca Maria Sforza, niece of Lodovico il Moro, and the second wife of Emperor Maximilian I.

19 bottom The castle of Forchtenstein, in Burgenland, was a stronghold in the resistance to Ottoman invasion. In the thirteenth century, it was highly prized among knights errant, largely because of the beauty of its chatelaine, the countess Tota von Mattersdorf.

Napoleon Bonaparte - four Emperors of Austria. All these mighty rulers must necessarily have left their mark, in the form of architecture and landscaping, amidst the forests, cities, and lakes of Austria.

This enormous and intricate network of power generated a mighty flow of trade, travel, art, and culture. Its effects can be seen on the facades of churches and palaces, libraries and art galleries. In no other way it is possible to comprehend the magnetic allure that so small a nation as the Republic of Austria continues to exercise, attracting tourists and generating some of the finest culture in the world. The bronze statuary of the impressive funerary structure that adorned the tomb of Maximilian I, in Innsbruck, was the joint effort of Albrecht Dürer and other excellent painters and sculptors, as well as master casters who travelled all the way from Sicily, bringing with them the secrets of the ancient Hellenistic founders of Magna Graecia.

Gattinara, who was the grand chancellor under Charles V, is buried in Innsbruck. In the church of the Minorite Order in Vienna - the church of the Italians - which stands directly behind the "House on the Ballhausplatz", the site of the imperial chancellery ever since the days of Metternich, there is a mosaic copy of Leonardo da Vinci's "Last Supper". The work was commissioned by Napoleon Bonaparte, who wished to be forgiven for certain of his grandiose pilferings. But by the time the mosaicist Giacomo Raffaelli had finished the work, Napoleon was being transported to his final and definitive exile on Saint Helena, and the bill was paid by the imperial treasury. The musical notes of the Flemish carillon built by Melchior van Hase hover over the seventeenth-century fountain, built by Tomaso da Cabona, in the Residenzplatz in Salzburg; all of which is not even to mention the blood ties. The two most powerful archbishops of Salzburg, Wolf Dietrich von Raitenau and Marcus Sitticus, were both related to the Borromeo family of Lombardy, Italy; hence the reverence in which St. Charles Borromeo is held, in Vienna and in other Austrian cities.

The House of Savoy, too, established extensive family ties with the House of Austria. The archduke Rainier, viceroy of Lombardy, married the young princess Elizabeth of Savoy, while Victor Emmanuel II married the archduchess Adelaide, the daughter of the same Rainier, although the "Gentleman King", as he was known, preferred the sweet company of *la bela Rosin* (the beautiful Rosin). His father, Charles Albert, had married the duchess Theresa of Hapsburg-Lorraine, the daughter of Ferdinand III, the grand-duke of Tuscany. And even Humbert I of Italy was intended as the groom in a wedding with an archduchess: Matilda of Hapsburg-Lorraine, who died in 1867 when she caught her camisole on fire while trying to conceal a smoking cigarette from her governess. Anne of Austria married Louis XIII of France, and Marie Antoinette married Louis XVI. The former was immortalised by Alexandre Dumas in "The Three Musketeers", where Anne is depicted as carrying on a flirtation with the duke of Buckingham.

The latter, of course, ended her life with considerable dignity under the blade of the guillotine. Extensive blood ties between the Hapsburgs and the house of Wittelsbach of Bavaria did little to improve the health

20 *Two views of Uno City, a major conference centre, that houses some of the organizations of the United Nations which have been scattered throughout Europe. It lies on the road that leads to Wagram, where Napoleon defeated the Austrians in a major battle in 1809. Not far away is the Alte Donau, a branch of the Danube that has been converted into a bathing resort. The quaint little church was built by Russian prisoners during the First World War.*

21 *The average Viennese is quite fond of his local tavern. Grinzing is one of the suburbs of the capital, along with Sievering and other locales scattered along the arc of the Wienerwald, or Vienna Woods. The taverns are called* Heurigen, *because originally vintners were authorised to sell their young wines for a brief period. They were required to* hang a branch from the house, in order to advertise that wine tasting was available. Today, these are full-fledged restaurants, often very nice ones, where the diners tend to break out in song. One of the old drinking songs went like this: "I smell a wine, miles away..."

22-23 *The Austrian countryside lends itself to great outings, hikes, and horseback riding, along narrow trails where automobiles cannot go. Countryside such as this, which is not far from Rauris in the Salzburg region, can be found all over Austria.*

24-25 *The enchanting little church of Maria Schnee (Mary of the Snows) stands at Garschurn on the slopes of the Silvretta, in Vorarlberg. It dates from the seventeenth century, but it has been renovated many times.*

of the dynasty.

Since every royal bride or groom brought into Austria with them, musicians, poets, architects, ladies-in-waiting, sculptors, and painters, their creations can be found on every hand - a truly staggering artistic patrimony. Whoever pauses to admire the little castle of Laxenburg, learns that it was built by Picassi.
At the Museum of Art History, there is a portrait of an emperor shaped like a basket of fruit, the work of Arcimboldo. The museum also owns works by Canaletto, Titian, Caravaggio, Velázquez, Vermeer, Brueghel, and Poussin. The country castles of Schönbrunn and Belvedere, and the palaces of Vienna bear the names of the aristocracy of all Europe: Lobkowitz, Pallavicini, Esterhazy, Cumberland, Eugene of Savoy, Trautson, Mollard-Clary, the Ladies of Savoy, Metternich, Rasumofsky, Schönborn-Batthiany.

The visitor thus finds himself gathered up and enveloped in, possibly without even realising it, what is called the Austrian atmosphere. It is an approaching to life relatively free of foreboding and concern about what might happen as a result. It is a cautious search for conciliation with the past, or at least an effort to be less dependent upon the present. Nostalgia? Perhaps not, because nostalgia is just a way of crippling the memory. Rather, it is an inclination to fatalism, deriving from the Slavic and Magyar components that have found their way into the Austrian blood and mindset. It can be said that every Austrian carries within his or her subconscious a bit of the wry cynicism of the good soldier Svejk, a portion of the unsettled thoughts of Young Törless, something of the lucid aftersight of Josef Roth, a link to the enchanted obedience of the Lords Trotta von Sipolje, an inclination or leaning toward what Robert Musil described as the man without qualities, and all the melancholy of Stefan Zweig, who committed suicide in Brazil in 1942.

A determination to think things through, combined with a carefree cheerfulness that does not disappear even in the presence of the ineluctable are the components of the Austrian mentality that are particularly striking; they appear as indulgence and unfailing courtesy. Karl Kraus, the most biting critical tongue in Vienna, used to savage the thoughtlessness of the Belle Epoque, a thoughtlessness that went hand in hand with the growing involvement of the Empire in that dangerous chain of conflict in the Balkans that was soon to explode in Sarajevo. Kraus called it a "carefree apocalypse". And Hugo von Hofmannsthal called it a "bubbly apocalypse". It is not easy to enter into this spirit. It was no accident that, both before and after the fall of the Berlin Wall, there should be a great and unending flow of refugees and renegades from the Balkans and Central Europe, which is to say, from the countries that once belonged to the Empire. Paradoxically, the capital of the little Austrian republic is once again linked in a network of interests and trade with the very same countries that once fought to escape from the iron grip of the Austro-Hungarian Empire; this time, however, without the dilemmas and the enormous costs of military subjugation and struggle.

In its multiplicity of physical types, in the babel of languages spoken in the street and in the workplace, in the variety of architectural styles, Vienna is a profoundly interesting city. The archetypes encountered here on a daily basis range from the Alemannic and Dinaric to the Longobard and Slavic; Italians live here in great numbers too. Both men and women are cosmopolitan in the finest sense of the word. The physiognomies are solid and robust in the countryside, finer and slimmer in the cities; blonde girls in casual dress, elderly women with an aristocratic appearance, and faces as disquieting as the models sketched by Gustav Klimt or Hans Makart.

In reference to the vast array of architectural styles, Vienna can truly be said to be a structural and stylistic melting pot, in part because of the original styles of the city's earliest development - from the Gothic to the Renaissance to the Baroque; and then because of the explosion of eclecticism that accompanied the construction of the Ring in the second half of the nineteenth century, when the Emperor, Franz Josef, decreed that the city walls should be torn down and that great boulevards be built, along with a majestic complex of handsome and well-proportioned buildings, including the state opera, the city hall, the parliament, the two great museums, the university, the stock exchange, and the various ministries. Here is a true triumph of eclecticism: post-gothic, post-baroque, neo-classical, hellenistic, romanesque, with early hints of biedermeier and art nouveau, in a harmonious array of shapes and elevations that can truly be considered unique.

In the heart of the venerable city centre, contained within the Ring, the ancient and the new coexist, though not always without squabbling. Two of the most recent cases of public controversy are these: first, the construction of a hypermodern commercial building where the Haas House once stood, in a corner of Sankt Stefan Platz; the second, more controversial still, is the case of the Hundertwasser House in the Löwenstrasse. This extremely modern building, which has been described with less than total accuracy as post-modern, is reminiscent in appearance of an airport control tower or the command superstructure of an aircraft carrier. This piece of modern architecture stands directly across the street from the imposing Gothic pile of the cathedral of St. Stephen's, and just a short distance away from the Pestsäule, the plague column, a remarkably baroque monument. But in its way, the Hundertwasser House is a particularly piercing cry of protest against the monotony of cement. This is a compound, polychrome building that combines in one structure a seemingly endless variety of styles, with cupolas, capitals, and terraces, a gleeful melange of Amalfi, Istanbul, with a dash of Tibetan monastery - a pastiche that the people of Vienna enjoy and admire. Its creator, the painter Friedensreich Hundertwasser, a mischievous character full of whimsical ideas, must have enjoyed himself immensely in designing and building it. Controversy is nothing new to Viennese architecture, and the controversy was perhaps at its fine roiling best when Otto Wagner and Adolf Loos were innovating away during the Secession and Art Nouveau. Even Emperor Franz Josef took part in the debate when Loos built the Goldmann House in St. Michael's Platz, directly across from the imperial residence, the Hofburg. The emperor described the stark and linear building as *das wimperlose Haus*, "the house without eyebrows".

22

Vienna is monumental and intimate at the same time. In the great square area enclosed as a pedestrian zone, bounded by the Käntnerstrasse, the Graben, the Kohlmarkt, St. Michael's Platz, the Augustinerstrasse, and the Albertina Platz, all of Vienna comes to meet and mingle. Here is the sublime Demel pastry shop, a temple to refined gluttony, bearing a sign that reads "K. & K. Hoflierferant" - "Purveyor to the Imperial Household" - and here are the stables of the Lipizzaner horses of the Spanish Riding School of the Imperial Court. Here are antiquarians and jewellers, the Dorotheum (a high-toned pawn shop with endless reserves of artworks and antique furniture in hock), and here is the little buffet of Trznjewski, where one can sample the very dangerous pepper tarts, marked with a red dot and a solemn warning: *Achtung Pfefferonen* - "Warning, Peppers". Behind the State Opera House are the two traditional coffee and pastry bars of the Hotel Sacher and the Café Mozart, with a little shop that will send the thoroughly traditional Sacher tortes anywhere in the world. Just a short distance away, beneath the walls of the Albertina, is an underground tavern where gentlemen and ladies often meet at the bar, drinking a glass of white wine from Burgenland or from the sweet southern slopes of the Wienerwald. The custom of taking a "drop of white" is an import from Lombardy and Venice. Count Joseph Radetzky, the Austrian field marshall, and former governor of Milan, used to do it himself.

In the austere and beautiful Josefsplatz, set between the National Library and the Palazzo Pallavicini, stands a tall and dignified statue of Emperor Joseph II, the favourite son of Maria Theresa. Joseph reigned jointly with his mother, when she was suffering from the asthma that would finally kill her, and was later the ruler of the empire. Joseph was an enlightened monarch who dared to decree in the late eighteenth century the abolition of those religious orders that did not either run hospitals or else perform some truly charitable work. The Jesuits and many other religious orders had to cease operations. The church has never truly forgiven him, but the people were pleased at the move. Not unlike Harun al Rashid, the Caliph of Baghdad, Joseph II would sometimes go out incognito to mingle with his people and to read their moods. One evening he entered a tavern on the Spittelberg, but the crowd immediately detected an outsider, and ejected him bodily.

Mozart considered Vienna to be "an excellent place to practise my profession, the best place in the world." A great many other noteworthy individuals have felt the same way: Franz Joseph Haydn, Burancini, Beethoven, the poet and librettist Pietro Metastasio, Sigmund Freud, the philosopher Ludwig Wittgenstein, and the psychiatrist Alfred Adler, men of the theatre, painters, musicians, and scientists. Even today, the theatres, concert houses, great museums, and libraries of Vienna are all world-class operations. The sumptuous parks, the muted atmosphere of the coffee shops, and the informal eateries are captivating. Many still find the lives of Franz Josef and Elizabeth particularly moving, especially in the context of a visit to the imperial residence of the Hofburg or to Schönbrunn. Some of the dramatic episodes are as follows: the homicide/suicide of the archduke Rudolf, the only son of Franz Josef and Elizabeth as well as heir to the throne, officially ruled a

double suicide, committed with his mistress Baroness Mary Vetsera, at Mayerling; the breakdown of the imperial marriage; Elizabeth's assassination in Geneva by the Italian anarchist Lucheni. "I am spared nothing," sighed the Emperor upon receiving the news. But worse was still to come, following the ultimatum to Serbia, which triggered World War I. But the Emperor mercifully died before the great defeat and the sad dissolution. His remains are buried in the crypt of the Capuchin Friars. Tourists are allowed to tour the place.

If, however, one wishes to spend an enjoyable evening in Vienna, without going to great theatres or to major concerts, one can go to the *Heurigen* in Grinzing or Sievering, unpretentious eateries with an enchantingly Viennese atmosphere. And if you are looking for excitement, there is the "Bermuda Triangle" near the venerable little church of St. Rupert, or else one can go to the Schönlaterngasse, near the old university and the Jesuit monastery, where young aristocrats were given acting lessons in the seventeenth century, so that they could acquire the behaviour of an *homme du monde*.

In this sort of atmosphere, the beauty of the landscape is no longer something that exists for its own sake - in the densest of forests a castle suddenly appears, in the white splendour of an Alpine valley a convent emerges, on the banks of the most tranquil of lakes a floating stage or a castle will appear. Salzburg requires a chapter of its own, because of its rare sumptuousness, the result of being a sort of Vatican amidst the mountains, with its architectural treasures and its musical heritage. The castles and the episcopal palaces that surround Salzburg document the earthly power of its archbishops, a power that was built upon salt mines and excommunications. Only the castle of Klessheim has a story all its own. The archduke Ludwig Victor, the younger brother of Franz Josef, was imprisoned there, after a scandal at the Diana Bad in Vienna.

Austria is a paradise for winter sports, and hordes of tourists and enthusiasts head for Carinthia, the Vorarlberg, the Tyrol, Styria, and the Salzburg region. Their time in these areas is made more pleasant by the presence of remarkable cities and towns, such as Graz, Klagenfurt, Villach, Innsbruck, Bregenz and Feldkirch - these are a pleasant bonus for those come in search of ski slopes and Alpine glaciers. In much the same way, during the summer, the profusion of great and lesser lakes scattered across the Austrian landscape is rendered more pleasant still by little resort towns such as Gmunden, with the castles on the Tuscan peninsula in the Salzkammergut; Eisenstadt, with the great Eszterhazy palace; Rust, in Burgenland; Velden or Pörtschach in Carinthia, or small resorts on Lake Constance. In this way, the villages are something more than a hotel and a place name. The prime attraction may still be the downhill racing at Sankt Anton or on the Hahnenkamm, the horse riding in Carinthia or Styria, the thrill of windsurfing, driven by the winds of the *puszta* or a windstorm out of Dachstein, causing navigational excitement worthy of Cape Horn. Nonetheless, these resort villages offer excursions into the past, into the spaces of history that can never be explored too thoroughly.

When the Mountain is Your Friend

26 top *Lech am Arlberg is the most important town in the Lechtal, as well as being an extremely popular centre for winter sports, as is the surrounding area - from Zürs all the way to the higher slopes of the Flexen Pass.*
The Arlberg massif, which once constituted an absolutely impassable obstacle during the winter, has become popular after the construction of the Arlberg railroad in the last century. Originally, stagecoaches would stop-over at Lech, and ever since the fourteenth century a little Gothic church, Sankt Nikolaus, offered shelter to lost wayfarers. The church still exists, although it has been modified.

26 bottom *The Alps of Kitzbühel, in the eastern Tyrol, offer one of the best known ski areas in the world.*
The downhill slope of Hahnenkamm is a landmark of Olympic gold and honours.

27 *Spring begins to stir in the limestone Alps of the Tyrol, near the lake of Achen and the village of Pertisau.*
The Achensee is almost six miles in length, and is about four hundred and thirty-five feet at its deepest. It is an ideal vacation spot for families of hikers.

A great respect for the outdoors

28-29 *The village of Schröcken, beneath the snow, in the Vorarlberg. This is a typical example of the great respect which Austrians have for nature. Buildings here - for the most part small hotels and pensions - have the traditional appearance of old farm houses. Here, the modern civilization of noise and frenzy is abolished. Architectural extravagance or idiosyncrasy is discouraged. Nothing is allowed to disturb the dignity of the mountains and the woods.*

When nature
unleashes its power

30-31 *In these photographs, the Grossglockner is enveloped by clouds twisted by the wind. This serves as a warning about the dangers that infest this mountain. The Grossglockner, whose name means the Great Bell-Ringer, is located in the mountains of the High Taurus, between the Tyrol and Carinthia. The Hochalpenstrasse* *(High Alpine Road) makes it possible to cross the mountain only during the season running from May to November. Over the mountain runs the glacier road, just grazing Pasterze and the great electrical power plant at Kaprun, with its enormous water basin. In the photograph on the right it is possible to see the Archduke John refuge.*

The High Tauri: plenty of "10,000" peaks

32-33 *On these pages, we see the mountain range of the High Taurus, which includes the famous and majestic peak of Grossglockner. The range is located partly in the Salzburg region and partly in the Tyrol, and includes over one hundred and twenty*

mountains, with peaks rising almost ten thousand feet. It reaches all the way to the Piz of the Three Men on the Italian border. A natural park covering more than three hundred and eighty-six square miles preserves the animals and vegetation of these remote areas.

34-35 *The colours of autumn illuminate the Möll valley, near Heiligenblut, in Carinthia. In the background rears the Grossglockner. Autumn is the "season of gold", when the foliage of ashes and oaks takes on the warm hues of burnished gold.*

36 top *Seefeld in the Tyrol is a handsome little town in the vast valley sheltered by the Karwendel mountain chain and the mountains of Wetterstein. In the little fifteenth-century church of Sant Oswald, there are remarkable frescoes that tell the story of the life of Saint Madeleine and the miracle of the Holy Host.*

36 bottom *Sankt Anton, on the Arlberg, is noted for its ski slopes. In the distant past, the village was a stop along the difficult route that linked the Tyrol with Switzerland and Lake Constance.*

37 *Hallstatt is an extremely charming village on the lake that bears the same name, in the Salzkammergut. The latter name means "Possessions of the Chamber of Salt"; rock-salt, in fact, was the chief resource here, along with the rich veins of silver. The region was under the rule of the archbishop princes of Salzburg and of the imperial family. During the nineteenth century, graves were found in the area surrounding the village, and anthropologists established that there had been a "Hallstatt civilization" that existed between the twelfth and the fifth centuries B.C.*

Just a stone's throw from Bavaria

38 The Hochkönig is another peak (9,646 feet) which towers over the Salzach river, after the stream has roared through the narrows of Sankt Veit in Pongau, and then winds toward Salzburg. Near the Hochkönig are the Hagengebirge and the Rock Sea mountain chain, whose ridges mark the boundary between Austria and Bavaria, toward the Königsee and Berchtesgaden. A remarkable downhill ski track leads from the peak of the mountain down to Bischofshofen on the river, a drop of 7,870 feet.

39 The highest peak in the Bavarian Alps is the Zugspitze 9,720 feet, standing in Tyrolean territory, not far from Leermos. Through a daring piece of engineering, a funicular links it with the little town of Obermoos; the seven-minute ride carries one upward 5,632 feet with just three pylons to support it. From the peak, one can enjoy a magnificent view of the Tyrolean Alps, all the way down to Cevedale in Italy. Near the station at the top of the funicular are a hotel and a restaurant with a little museum. From there, it is possible to walk to the German refuge called Münchner Haus, and then to climb down towards Bavaria, to the Eibsee.

40 Bad Gastein would never have become famous had Duke Frederick of Styria not gone there to take the waters at the local thermal springs, curing a wound that had begun to gangrene. For four centuries, the springs brought fame but little more, until the beginning of the twentieth century when the Emperor Franz Josef inaugurated the Taurus Tunnel, five miles in length. As soon as the shuttle train began operations, the entire valley developed a resort economy. Alongside Bad Gastein, the more affordable resorts of Bad Hofgastein and Dorfgastein sprang up. The social activity of these places is documented by the luxurious hotels and the stories of princes, princesses and spies that hover over the valley. In the foreground is the chapel of Saint Anna.

41 The Augustine abbey of Göttweig was founded back in 1074, and over time extensive renovations were done by Johann Lucas von Hildebrandt and Cesare Biagino. The abbey stands in the Wachau, on the right bank of the Danube, across from Krems, in a location midway between the abbeys of Melk and Klosterneuburg. The complex of buildings is luxurious in its baroque splendour, set atop the ancient foundations and the Gothic walls. As early as the thirteenth century, a cloistered nun, Ava von Gottweig, wrote a collection of poetry in the convent. Her work was considered to be the forerunner of Austrian chivalric poetry.

42-43 The woods of Austria abound in wildlife and game. Hunting regulations are rather strict and hunters cannot get a licence without taking an examination. Mountain goats and stags are abundant, as are wild boar and other smaller game. The animals are protected from hunting during the season of the snows, during mating season, and while the females are bearing their young.

44-45 The massif of Dachstein rises to the south of Hallstatt, towering over the lake of the same name, directly across from the entrance to the ancient mine from which rock-salt was quarried. This mountain is an enormous pile of boulders that rises to 8,000/9,500 feet; it is considered particularly dangerous because of the bad weather and raging mountain storms that strike without the slightest warning. This photograph shows clearly how the clouds come pouring down the mountain gorges, often without any advance indication. At about halfway up the mountain, on the side nearest Obertraun, one can enter the famous ice caverns, a tourist attraction of remarkable interest because of the freakish and bizarre structures that are created by the alternately dripping of melting water and the slow accretion of frozen water. At the foot of the Dachstein there are celebrated rock-climbing schools.

46-47 *The Krimmler Wasserfalle is one of the most beautiful waterfalls in the Alps. The waters that rush down from the mountainous group of the Grossvenediger and flow into the river Salzach run over a series of drops in the area around the town of Krimml, descending a total of 1,250 feet. The average volume of the stream is 2,650 gallons per second. During the thaw, or when heavy rains have fallen, the volume can increase to 103,350 gallons per second. From the Schönangerl eatery, the view can be simply terrifying.*

Amidst horses and castles

48 *It is quite common to encounter horses in Austrian countryside. Tractors cannot get through everywhere, and so in some situations horses are preferred. For the most part, these are Haflinger horses, or horses of the Nordic breeds, light high-tempered draft horses, often nicely dappled.*

49 *The massive castle of Hohenwerfen looms above the town of Werfen, and straddles the course of the river Salzach upstream from Salzburg, in a strategic point on the border separating the old archbishop's principality of Salzburg from Bavaria.*

Folkore, and More

50-51 *Traditional clothing, known as* Trachten, *is often worn in villages and in the countryside. For work clothing, leather shorts or breeches, known as* Lederhosen *or* Pumphosen, *are usual in the fields. Women's outfits are usually worn on religious occasions. Men also wear traditional jackets during social events. In this case, the* jackets with red or green pipestem lapels, often decorated with oak leaf motifs, are called Alpensmoking, meaning Alpine dinner jackets. In the Austrian cities, on the other hand, women often wear the dirndl, *a dress commonly made of colourful and strikingly patterned material, especially brocades.*

Here come
the Schützen

52-53 *The Schützen form part of an old institution, half civilian and half military. In mountain villages, where almost all of the men are hunters, and where in the past the concept of self-defence was automatic and instinctive, these associations of sharpshooters sprang up of their own accord, solidifying their structure each year with shooting contests and with competitions between marching bands. When Napoleon invaded, the Schützen became particularly powerful in the Tyrol.*

After the war, the Schützen also became associations of veterans. In this photograph, we see a band from the Tyrol, and one of the band-members, wearing medals from World War Two.

Carnival, no holds barred

54   *Carnival masks vary from region to region. In general, carnival in Austria is celebrated with great masked celebrations. The* Schemenlaufen *of Imst in the Tyrol are particularly famous. The various masked figures may be silent or noisy, austere or wild dancers. The* Tuxer, *shown in the photograph, is a propitiatory mask covered with flowers and budding branches. The* Zottler *are pairs of harlequin-like figures that dance and make a tremendous amount of noise.*

54-55   *Masked processions are generally quite noisy and chaotic. The masks have ancient religious origins, and can be divided into three broad categories. The word mask comes from the Longobard term* masca, *which indicated the netting in which corpses were once shrouded. When the body was buried, the netting was taken by the evil spirits, who were thus mollified. The* schemae, *from the Greek for "shadow" are masks that represent phantoms or ghosts.* Larvae - *related to the Latin term* lares, *meaning ancestor - are good, benevolent ghosts. To these masks are added devils, bears, witches, and in the end a dizzying confusion is guaranteed.*

56 *The procession of the* Perchten
*wends its way through the streets of Bad
Gastein. The participants, wearing
heavy flowered headgear, are the
followers of the terrible Lady Percht.
She is a demonic creature, and her
followers, who behave in the most
reasonable of manners - at least in part
because they are quite occupied in
balancing their heavy flowered
headgear - are there only to exorcise the
bad spirits and evil deeds of their
leader.*

57 top *A group of* Zottler *moves towards the site of the procession in orderly rank and file. When they enter into action, they will dance in pairs, and those who are in the neighborhood had better be careful!*

57 bottom *Salzburg devils head off for more devilry. The* Teufelsrummel *comes before Carnival. It takes place on the evening of 6 December, on the occasion of the feast of Saint Nicholas. As terrible as their appearances may be, the devils behave in a good-natured manner, making noise and sometimes drinking from the glasses of others. In order to drink, however, they must remove their heads. Thus, one might see a devil quaffing a beer with his head on a table nearby - not unlike a Saint John after his decapitation.*

58 *The propitiatory festivals of Spring are far more gentle and refined than the carnival celebrations. At Bad Aussee, in the Salzburg region, boats are bedecked with flowers and then are sailed in an aquatic procession to win the good will of deities that populate the lakes with fish. These are clearly rituals of pagan origin, and they may derive from Nordic sagas. The modern touch is there - the flower-decked boats are driven by outboard motors.*

59 *The Feast of the Narcissus takes place at Bad Aussee, on the shores of the Grundlsee. Here young girls braid ring dances, carrying a garland of narcissus in honour of the Goddess Ostara, the earliest adminstrator of the wealth of the earth and the benefits of the same. The music that accompanies this event is generally quite folksy: accordions, zithers, and other odd mountaineer instruments, such as a sort of bass made of tin in the shape of a female body. This type of instrument is fairly common in the peasant festivals of Alpine Austria.*

60 top *In this picture, one can admire a phase of the procession of Sankt Veil in eastern Tyrol.*

60 bottom *At the beginning of the wheat harvest, the peasants of Carinthia make allegorical figures and trophies out of the sheaves of wheat, which they carry in a procession to the church. This is a repetition of the ancient rite of the* part Dieu, *which is to say, of the part of the products that the earth gives to the family that is reserved to God.*

61 *During the spring festivals, or during the festival of the patron saint, on* Kirchtag, *or Church Day, the peasants wear traditional costumes. This woman from the Traunsee area wears a finely embroidered bonnet - known as* Haube. *The Traunsee, in the Salzburg area, is rich in historical and romantic tradition.*

Vienna, the Grandeur of the Empire

62 *The summer residence of Schönbrunn was built by Maria Theresa towards the middle of the eighteenth century. The residence was planned by Fischer von Erlach, one of the founding figures of Austrian Baroque. The architect called for a complex of buildings and other fittings in the park, which was meant to outshine the palace of Versailles, pride and joy of Louis XIV. The empress, however, soon realised that the cost would be astronomical, and she settled for what we see now. In the photograph at the top we see the Gloriette, which dominates the castle and the park from atop a lovely hill. At the bottom, we see the majestic rear facade of the castle.*

63 *The new Hofburg is the most recently built wing of the Imperial Palace in Vienna. On the first floor, on the horse in the levade position, there is a statue of Prince Eugene of Savoy, Count of Soissons, who definitively crushed the Turkish invasion.*

64-65 *The neo-Gothic town hall of Vienna, built in 1870 on the Ring, to plans by the architect Friedrich Schmidt, is a loud but imposing structure that is in some ways reminiscent of the town hall of Brussels. The interiors are sufficiently luxurious, and the ballroom has a floor space of over twelve hundred square yards. In the hall, there are giant statues of great historical figures.*

In the square of Maria Theresa

66 *The monument to Maria Theresa claims pride of place in the centre of the square, with a splendid effect of perspective. Beyond the Ring stands the entrance gate to the Hofburg and the Heroes Square, with equestrian monuments to Prince Eugene of Savoy and the Archduke Charles. The monument depicts the Empress seated on her throne, elevated upon a pedestal at the corners of which are statues of the four statesmen and generals who served her during her reign.*

67 *The building of the Museum of Art History and its twin, the Museum of Natural History, stand on either side of the monument to Maria Theresa in a balanced architectural harmony. The former, in particular, has one of the wealthiest collections in Europe.*

68-69 *The general view of Vienna from the bell tower of Saint Stephen's church clearly shows the magnificence of the capital. In the foreground, one can see the cupolas of the Saint Michael wing of the imperial palace and the tall sharp bell tower of the church of Saint Michael. The Hellenistic colonnade on the right is the pronaos of parliament.*

The Emperor opens Parliament

70 *The building of the Austrian parliament was designed by the Danish architect Theophil Hansen, and built over a period of ten years, between 1873 and 1883. The building is a celebratory monument: the relief on the pediment depicts the Emperor Franz Josef gathering in parliament the seventeen territories of the crown. The statue of Minerva was the work of Karl Kundmann.*

71 top *At the foot of the columns are marble statues of great lawmakers and philosophers of the past. In the foreground is Thucydides, the great historian, with a scroll of his "History of the Peloponnesian War."*

71 bottom *The neo-Hellenistic parliament building is truly imposing. The total ground area is nearly four acres, but the building is so perfectly proportioned that it does not seem particularly colossal. The immense entrance staircase is adorned by two bronze statues of horse tamers. The pediment is crowned with sixty statues of figures from ancient Greece and Rome. Inside, the Hall of Columns and the reception hall possess a majesty that only the world of antiquity can rival.*

The churches of the capital

72 The main facade of the cathedral of Saint Stephen is a handsome example of central European Gothic architecture. The cathedral is set upon the base of a Romanesque church dating from the thirteenth century, which was destroyed by a fire. During the worst fighting at the end of the Second World War, the roof covering -- both nave and transept -- was burnt and collapsed inside the church. The pulpit of Capistrano is particularly interesting, as is a bust of Jesus which the Viennese call "Christ with a Toothache", because of the grimace that is distorting the features of the Saviour. The Pummerin, the historical bell of the cathedral, which also fell into the nave at the end of the war, was not successfully restored to its bell tower until 1957. The Viennese call their cathedral "Steffi", which is a nickname for Stephen.

73 The Karlskirche, a church dedicated to St. Charles Borromeo, is one of the most sumptuous baroque buildings in the capital of Austria. Work on the church began in 1716, under the Austrian architect Johann Bernhard Fischer von Erlach; it was completed in 1737 by the architect's son Johann Emmanuel. The monumental central structure and the classical pronaos, on the pediment of which appears the legend in relief - "Disasters of the Plague" - are flanked by two triumphal columns in the finest Roman style, with a spiralling narrative of the life of St. Charles Borromeo. The interior of the church is harmonious and full of light, decorated with frescoes by Johann Rottmayr von Rosenbrunn. On the central altar there is a great marble statue of the Holy Trinity.

Life at court

74 *The tour of the imperial apartments in the old Hofburg, which is open to the public, is particularly interesting. The palace, which was the residence of the Hapsburgs from 1283 until 1918, is a vast complex of buildings structured around the so-called Schweizer Hof, or the Courtyard of the Swiss, which dates from the reign of king Otakar II Przemisl of Bohemia. Each wing of the palace has a name - the Michaelertrakt, which looks out over the square of Saint Michael, is a truly magnificent wing, with two monumental fountains, representing the two realms, maritime and terrestrial. In the top and centre photographs, it is possible to admire two halls in the imperial apartments. The painting in the centre depicts Franz Josef.*

74 bottom *The imperial banquet table in this photograph is richly laden. In reality, however, Franz Josef was a man of fairly simple tastes, who actually preferred to sleep on an iron cot.*

75 *Prince Eugene of Savoy, who beat the Turks at Passarowicz, was the son of a member of the Savoy-Carignano family and of Olympia Manicini, the niece of Cardinal Mazarin, and an old lover of Louis XIV. The prince was turned down by the Sun King when he asked to command a regiment of Dragoons, because he was quite short. So the young count of Soissons turned to the Hapsburgs, pursuing a splendid career as a general and as a warrior. In the background, one can see the colonnade of the Neue Hofburg, the new wing of the imperial palace.*

Going around with Herr Kutscher

76 top *The Burgtheater, on the Ring, was founded as a theatre of the Imperial Court; when the Republic was founded, it was left with the status of a castle. This is the premiere theatrical venue in Austria, a land with an ancient and deep-rooted tradition of stage performance. The Burgtheater is the leading theatre in Vienna.*

76 centre *The Graben, or pedestrian zone, is the heart of Vienna, along with the Kärntnerstrasse and the Kohlmarkt. At the centre of this zone stands the Pestsäule, a flamboyant votive column designed by Johann Bernhard Fischer von Erlach and Ottavio Burancini as a sign of thanksgiving for the end of an outbreak of the plague.*

76 bottom *The Majolika Haus in the Linke Wienzeile is one of the buildings designed by the Austrian architect Otto Wagner, one of the most respected figures in the Vienna Secession of the turn of the century. The idea of using ceramics was a way of making modern houses stronger and longer lasting.*

77 *The horse cab is called a* Fiaker *and the cab driver is addressed as* Herr Kutscher, *meaning "Mr. Cab Driver". The horses have all sorts of names, ranging from the illustrious names of emperors and empresses of Austria's past to the more modest names, such as Pubi and Marko. The main horse cab stands in Vienna are found in St. Stephen's Square (Stephansplatz) and in Josefplatz.*

78 Few cities in the world can boast such illustrious composers as Vienna: Mozart, Beethoven, Schubert, Mahler, Berg, Bruckner, von Webern, Schönberg, which is not even to mention the "lightweights" - the Strausses, Millöcker, Lehar - For a century, titanic battles have been waged between those in favour of harmony and those in favour of atonal music, though waltzes were danced and tunes from operettas were hummed all the while. Wolfgang Amadeus Mozart, the young man from Salzburg, remains the composer dearest to the hearts of the Austrians, however. The monument to Mozart in the Burggarten also records his exchange with the emperor Joseph II. The evening of the presentation of "The Abduction from the Serraglio", Joseph II said to the composer: "Too many notes, Herr Mozart". "Just enough, Your Majesty", the composer answered.

A city for music

79 left *Franz Schubert was a great but unfortunate composer. Nonetheless, a monument to Schubert was erected in the Stadtpark, and his house was made into a museum. Moreover, while walking through the streets of Vienna, it is common to hear people humming and whistling strains from Schubert's work.*

79 right *No doubt, the greatest figure of the Belle Epoque was certainly Johann Strauss. The monument to Strauss in the Stadtpark depicts him as he was: slender, elegant, ambitious, curly-locked, with coy moustachioes: "Vienna: Wine, Women, and Songs."*

The castle of
Prince Eugene

80-81 *The Belvedere was built to plans by Josef Lucas von Hildebrandt in the first quarter of the eighteenth century. From 1904 until the assassination in Sarajevo, this was the residence of the archduke Francis Ferdinand who, however, because of his morganatic marriage to Sophie Chotek, lived in Moravia, far from the imperial court. In the salon of honour, in 1955, the so-*

called State Treaty was signed, establishing that the Allied Powers were restoring Austria to its sovereign and independent status, provided that the country declare itself to be neutral in the future.

The last century of the Empire

82 *The nineteenth century was a time of greatness and decay for Austria. This was the century of eclecticism, a period of intense social pressures and of nationalistic conflict. It was a century of cultural progress and a time of repression, an era of huge investments and of injustice, of magnificence and of dissipation. When Franz Josef in 1860 had the walls of Vienna torn down, replacing them with the Ring, he triggered a construction boom hitherto inconceivable, the results of which are still a source of city pride. That was when the famous statement was made: "When construction is booming the entire economy is booming." Whether the things that were built at that time were beautiful and on a human scale can be judged by the viewer on the basis of this photograph of the parliament and its statues.*

83 *This photograph of Vienna shows us the area around the Ring. Against the backdrop of the baroque dome of the Museum of Art History, the figure of Maria Theresa, the wise and enlightened empress, appears in all its serenity. An expert in photography will easily note that, since the statue of the* *empress stands a good two hundred and sixty feet from the Museum building, the type of lens used here is fundamental. Of equal importance is the precision of the planners in creating this sort of urban furnishing that remains impeccable and attractive after more than a century.*

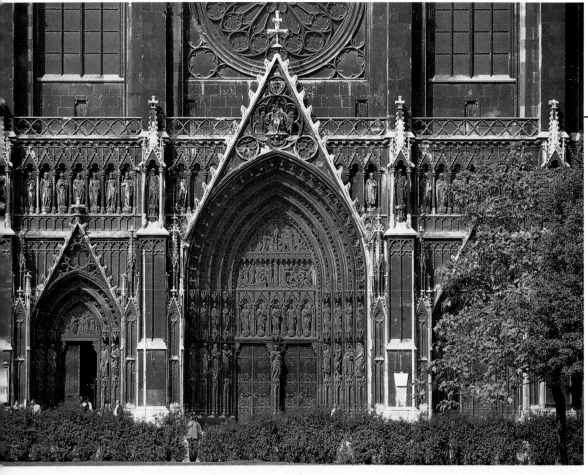

An Emperor
gives thanks

84 *The Votivkirche was built at the orders of the Emperor Franz Josef in thanksgiving for his survival of an assassination attempt. The Votivkirche stands on the spot where an Hungarian tailor tried to kill him in 1853. The church was designed by the architect Heinrich Ferstel, who took his inspiration from French Gothic architecture of the thirteenth century. The church, which has three naves and two bell towers that stand three hundred and thirty feet tall is a masterpiece of workmanship, though it is architecturally an imitation. We see the portal in this photograph.*

84 bottom *The interesting workmanship of the stone carvers can be seen clearly on the balustrade of the Votivkirche, or Votive Church. It is worth pointing out that, during the decade or so in which they worked on the church, Austria suffered defeat at the hands of the Prussians at Sadowa-Königgrätz, even though Austria had also beaten the Italians at Custoza and Lyssa. As an overall result of the war of 1866, Austria remained under the subjugation of Prussia, as well as subject to the incessant pressure of trouble with Hungary.*

85 *The Votivkirche looks out over the Sigmund Freud Park, right at the intersection of the Schotten Ring and Dr. Karl Lüger Ring, not far from the Alma Mater, the central campus of the University, in an airy and sunny location, which helps to emphasise the elegance of the construction.*

Authentic baroque
and romantic style

86 *The National Library, overlooking
the square dedicated to Emperor Joseph
II, is a building of serene magnificence,
crowned by two groups of sculptures:
"Minerva on Her Chariot", on the
central structure, and "Gea Holding
the Terrestrial Sphere and Atlas with
the Celestial Sphere", on either wing.
The sculptures are the work of Ludovico
Mattinelli (1726). The library was
built at the order of Emperor Charles
VI, and possesses, among other things,
the Prunksaal, or Gala Hall, shown in
this photograph.*

87 top *This picture shows the Clock
Museum. Vienna possesses an
astonishing array of small specialty
museums; among them is even an
Undertakers' Museum.*

87 bottom *The library is set in the
body of the Hofburg, and its catalogue
numbers some seven million items,
including books, incunabula, prints,
manuscripts, and documents of all sorts.
The collection was begun by Emperor
Frederick III, father of Maximilian I.*

88-89 *The architect Heinrich Ferstel
built the palace that bore his name as
an experiment in Romantic architecture,
between the Herrengasse and the Freyung
in 1855. A glassed-in passage and an
interior courtyard-patio connect the two
streets. Originally, the place housed the
headquarters of the Austro-Hungarian
Bank. Today, it houses the Café Central
and other venerable institutions.*

90-91 *The Prater also forms part of the legends of the Vienna. This is a huge amusement park, with beer gardens, vendors of cotton candy, a giant ferris wheel with fourteen cabins, a haunted castle, shooting galleries, funhouse mirrors... This is just a tiny part of the immense tree-lined estate built on the so-called Donau-Auen, the destination for pleasant strolls and horseback rides. The principal boulevard is three miles in length. Here and there are little lakes which in winter become skating rinks. At the end of the boulevard is a pavilion which has also become famous. One can reach the Prater from the Praterstern, the square in the Leopoldstadt, the neighbourhood beyond the Canal of the Danube. In the Praterstern, there is a column dedicated to Admiral Tegetthof, the victor at the battle of Lyssa.*

Coffee, wine, women and song

92 *This picture shows the interior of the historical Café Central. Cafés are one of the most pleasant of all Austrian traditions. People meet at the café, they read newspapers, they write, they discuss business. The first café in Vienna was opened by a Pole, a certain Kolschitzki, who had stolen a number of bags from the Turks. He thought that those bags contained forage for camels, but instead they contained coffee. Other famous cafés include the Heinrichshof, the Griendsteidl, and the Museum, in the Sezession Haus by Adolf Loos, which Emperor Franz Josef called "the house without eyebrows", because of its bare, unadorned windows.*

93 *Inns and Heurigen, or wine gardens, are particularly beloved of the Viennese, both in the outskirts of town and in the centre. The setting is unpretentious: benches and rough tables allow one to sit solidly; much wine leads to discussion and singing. Beethoven was very fond of the Heurigen of Grinzing and Döbling. Schubert frequented an inn in the centre of Vienna, which still exists, in the passageway from the archbishop's palace and the Diocese Museum.*

The pleasure of the chill

94 *Strolling through parks and gardens under a blanket of snow creates a sense of serenity. The snow covers buildings and statues, as can be seen in this photograph taken from the upper square of the Belvedere, the secondary residence of the prince, Eugene of Savoy.*

95 *The skating rink on Lothringerstrasse is heavily used during the winter, in part because of its convenient location. At times, there are hundreds of skaters shooting along to the tune of a waltz or a local ditty. The grey building is the Konzerthaus, where the Akademie Theatre is based. The dome in the background is that of the Karlskirche.*

Lippizaners
and Debutantes

96 *The famous Spanish Riding School of the Austrian Court is one of the country's traditional institutions, a legacy of the time when Austria and Spain were both ruled by Hapsburgs. The riding school is in the Michaelertrakt wing of the Hofburg.*

96-97 *The Debutantes' Ball at the State Opera House is one of the great annual events in Austria's - and Europe's - better social circles, because young men and women from other countries can take part as well. The atmosphere is typically Viennese:* *the participants drink champagne, but they also eat Vienna sausages, which are called Frankfurter here, not to honour the German city on the Main river, but because the butcher who first "invented" them was called Frankfurter.*

The Smaller Cities

98 top *Innsbruck, the capital of the Tyrol, has a history that stretches into the distant past. The city's earliest origins, in fact, date from the Bronze Age; with the advent of the Romans, the city was named Veldidena, while the current name dates from 1180, after the town established itself with a new status near a bridge over the river Inn.*

98 bottom *The Herrengasse in Graz, the capital of Styria, led an existence that was relatively unfettered by connections with Vienna. This was largely due to the personality of Duke Charles of Styria, whose descendents later took the imperial throne when the direct line died out, since neither Rudolf II nor his brother Matthias had children. This photograph shows the Herrengasse, an important street in the city.*

99 *With its sumptuous and intimate nature, Salzburg reminds one of a backdrop for an opera. Its prosperity was based, over the centuries, upon the monopoly on salt which its archbishop-princes enjoyed. This is the city of Mozart, whose father was the second kapellmeister to the archbishop. The composer left Salzburg following a dispute with the archbishop Colloredo. This photograph shows the fortress of Salzburg that overlooks the city with its imposing walls and fortifications. To the right one can see the building of the Festival, with its bronze lion, situated before the bell tower of the church of Saint Francis.*

Salzburg, baroque harmony

100-101 *The river Salzach splits Salzburg into two parts. On the left bank is the old city, with the castle, the cathedral, and the Residence. On the opposite bank (picture on the right), is the new part of the city.*

102-103 *Salzburg has an extremely ancient history. Founded by the Illyrians, who built a fortified village upon the Mönchsberg - or Mountain of the Monks - the site was later taken over by the Romans, under Emperor Claudius, who established the* oppidum *of Iuvavum. It*

was Saint Rupert, the bishop of Worms, who gave Salzburg its modern name of "City of Salt". Run for centuries by the clergy, during the Counter Reformation Salzburg became a major cultural centre linking Bavaria with the regions of Austria, and the archbishop-princes impressed upon it its sumptuous nature. Napoleon made this a secular power in 1802, and it was later annexed to Austria after the Congress of Vienna.

105 top left *The quaint Getreidegasse,
upon which stands the house in which
Wolfgang Amadeus Mozart was born,
is invariably crowded.*

104 *The Archbishop's Palace, or Old
Residence, was built between 1596 and
1619 on the site it occupied in the
Middle Ages, and is distinguished by its
numerous halls, lavishly decorated and
furnished. The Residenzbrunner, which
stands at the centre of the square, was
created by the Italian artist, Tomaso da
Cabona, and is the largest and most
highly regarded baroque fountain
outside of Italy. The square is often
lined with carriages, a comfortable and
enjoyable way of getting around town.*

105 top right *The drinking trough for
horses - the Pferdschwemme - is a
magnificent fountain built alongside
the old summer riding school and the
Festspielhaus, or Festival Hall, built
into the solid rock of the Mönchsberg.*

105 bottom *The statue of Mozart
stands alongside the Mozarteum in
eastern Salzburg. In this area also
stands the house to which the Mozart
family repaired after leaving their
residence in the Getreidegasse.*

106-107 *The Salzburg area attracts enormous numbers of tourists, some of them lovers of fine music, but many of them fans of winter sports, or merely lovers of nature. This view of Zell am See, a village located to the south of Salzburg, on the banks of a charming little lake, shows the comfortable atmosphere that prevails in most ski resorts in Austria.*

108 *The castle of Mirabell has been the summer residence of the archbishop-princes ever since 1606. It was renovated by Lucas von Hildebrandt in 1725 and it is surrounded by a spectacular park. In the hall of honour is a marble Perseus by Antonio Canova, adorned by bronze cherubs, the work of Donner. In one of the greenhouses of the castle is a Museum of the Baroque.*

109 *The castle of Hellbrunn was the summer residence of the archbishop Marcus Sitticus. This is an elegant seventeenth-century building surrounded by a grandiose park, in which cheerful water sculptures have been created. Sitticus must have had a mischievous personality, since the water jets do not merely startle the guests, but actually douse them thoroughly when they are sitting down to dinner.*

Innsbruck, the bridge over the river Inn

110 *The Goldenes Dachl, or house of the Golden Roof, at Innsbruck, was built by order of the Emperor Maximilian I in a residential palace belonging to his father, Friedrich, and his uncle, Sigismund, known as "Rich in Money", because he owned silver mines in Schwaz. The roof is covered with gilded plates, and on the panels of the balustrade there appear depictions of the two wives of Maximilian, Marie of Bourgogne and Bianca Maria Sforza.*

111 *The triumphal arch in Maria Theresienstrasse commemorates the visit of the Empress to Innsbruck. The capital of the Tyrol was for centuries a stronghold of the Hapsburgs, and the city contributed more than any other to support the exploits of Maximilian. The name of Innsbruck indicates the function of the city - "Bridge on the Inn".*

111 left *The historical centre of Innsbruck is essentially built around a series of elegant buildings and homes dating from the seventeenth and eighteenth centuries, with loggias or jutting windows.*

112-113 *The Annasäule, or Anna column, was erected in 1706 in Maria Theresienstrasse to commemorate the retreat of Bavarian forces in the War of Spanish Succession. Upon the column are marble statues of Saint Ann and other patron saints of Tyrol.*

114 *The Herzog Friedrichstrasse is the most distinctive street in Innsbruck, with its low mediaeval porticoes. In the background, it is possible to see the Goldenes Dachl, or house of the Golden Roof. The buildings date from the fifteenth and sixteenth centuries, and have been re-frescoed during recent years. The bell tower that can be seen in the centre of the picture belongs to the Church of Saint Jacob.*

115 *Overall view of the centre of town, from the tower of city hall. The houses present the distinctive features of late Gothic and early Renaissance style. The bell tower belongs to the church of the Servite Order.*

116 top *The palace of the Residence stands just a short distance from the river Inn, near the cathedral. Here the Dukes of the Tyrol held court, even later, when they had become the rulers of the Holy Roman Empire.*

116 right *In the court chapel, which shares its entrance with the Provincial Museum, the cenotaph of Maximilian I can be seen. The funerary shrine is surrounded by an imposing group of bronze statues, of exquisite workmanship. These statues depict the ancestors - real and imagined - of the Hapsburg family. Some of these figures were designed by Albrecht Dürer. Maximilian, however, is not buried here, but at Wiener Neustadt.*

116 centre *The Altstadt, the historical centre, is marked by a number of different styles: Tyrolian architecture can be seen in such features as the pitch*

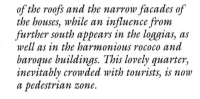

of the roofs and the narrow facades of the houses, while an influence from further south appears in the loggias, as well as in the harmonious rococo and baroque buildings. This lovely quarter, inevitably crowded with tourists, is now a pedestrian zone.

116 bottom *In the middle of the Maria Theresienstrasse, in front of the Town Hall, stands the Annasaeule, the "Column of Saint Ann", erected in 1706 to express thanksgiving for the withdrawal of Bavarian troops in 1703, on Saint Ann's Day.*

116-117 *The court and the various religious buildings are directly adjacent or, in any case, quite close to the city centre, so that certain streets, such as the Herzog Heinrich Strasse, are thronged with souvenir shops, small bars, cafés, and wine-tasting rooms.*

118 The Hungerburgbahn is a combined funicular and cable car that runs from Innsbruck over to the left bank of the Inn, and then on up to the castle of Weiherburg, and the stations of the cable car that runs to Seegrube. A detour leads to the historic castle of Absam. To the south of Innsbruck, on the other hand, is the hill where Igls stands, with its little castle and its Olympic ski jump.

119 The Inn valley divides the mountains of the Limestone Alps and the Karwendel to the north, from the Alps of Tux and of Zillerthal to the south. On the right bank of the river, a few miles downstream from Innsbruck, is the little town of Schwaz, which possesses an interesting fifteenth-century church. Not far from Schwaz is the so-called hill of silver. In the three hundred miles of tunnels that have been dug into the mountain lay the great wealth of Sigismund "Wealthy in Coins" and of Maximilian I. The silver mines can be toured, with an interesting system of lighting and of guides.

120-121 The mediaeval castle of Ambras, formerly owned by the Andachs, was destroyed by Bavarian troops in 1133, and rebuilt a century-and-a-half later, on the same site. Stronghold of the Hapsburgs ever since the reign of Frederick III and his son Maximilian, it later became their residence as well. The castle houses a museum of arms and armour, whose collection includes the burnished suit of armour of Francis II Gonzaga. Among the firearms in the museum, there are cannons captured from the Turks, with names such as "The Turkish Empress", and "The Abominable Lion". The artistic collections of the Hall of Art and Wonders are of particular interest.

FERDINANDUS II ARCHIDUX AUSTRIAE

Graz, a city made to human dimensions

122 top *In terms of population, Graz, capital of Styria, is the second largest city in Austria. Set in a verdant location overlooking the Mur River, which runs gently amidst the hilly countryside, this is the home city of the Leopoldine line, which took power after the Tyrolean line of the Hapsburg family died out. The enormous castle gives some evidence of the power and wealth of the Styrian line, which was based in this city for three centuries, before moving to Vienna.*

122 bottom *Graz is surmounted by a picturesque hill called the Schlossberg, or Mountain of the Castle, and it was occupied three times by the soldiers of Napoleon Bonaparte. The old main square, surrounded by venerable buildings, still hosts a cheerful flower, fruit and vegetable market.*

123 *The parish church on the Herrengasse has a beautiful baroque facade dating from the early eighteenth century, and is surrounded by interesting buildings on all sides, including the famous "Painted House" and the Breuner Palace. The sixteenth-century headquarters of the provincial government was built by Domenico d'Allio. The arsenal building was designed by Antonio Solari. The Provincial Museum is wealthy and interesting, and is known as the Johanneum; it was named after the archduke John, who was made an honorary citizen of Graz.*

124-125 *The Landhaus, the regional hall of Graz, has an elegant renaissance style. In the enormous courtyard with its three orders of arcades, public concerts are frequently held, as are other theatrical performances.*

The pleasant villages of Carinthia

126 *Klagenfurt, the capital of Carinthia, is a small city linked by a short canal to the Wörther See. The rivers Glan and Gurk run nearby, and thus the residents of the city can indulge in fishing as well as hunting. The great structure of the cathedral was built by Protestants at the end of the sixteenth century, and later incorporated into a Jesuit convent. The Jesuits saw to its furnishing with baroque sumptuousness. During the war, the convent was partially destroyed.*

127 top *Klagenfurt is a city with a tranquil lifestyle, dotted with tree-lined squares and handsome, Biedermeier houses. The Landhaus, a noble, renaissance construction, is particularly interesting.*

127 bottom *Villach is a small city in Carinthia that is every bit as tranquil as the capital. The city is frequented by tourists on their way to and from the Wörther See, and the attractive resorts of Velden and Rörtschach. Tradition has it that the dragon of Villach twitches its tail if a virgin walks by. "That tail has never moved", say the merchants in the town square.*

128 *The antique sign of a Heuringen at Grinzing. Beneath the imperial eagle are purveyed local foods, sweets, and music.*